The Gang's All Here

Mary Waesche Alessi
Cathy Fosnot

Illustration by Manuela Pentangelo

We dedicate this book to our children and grandchildren, who continually stimulate and challenge us to keep our minds creative.

"Ugh, I hope these chicks come soon," Loretta Leghorn thought to herself. "It's like sitting on a bunch of hard lumpy rocks. My bottom is sore."

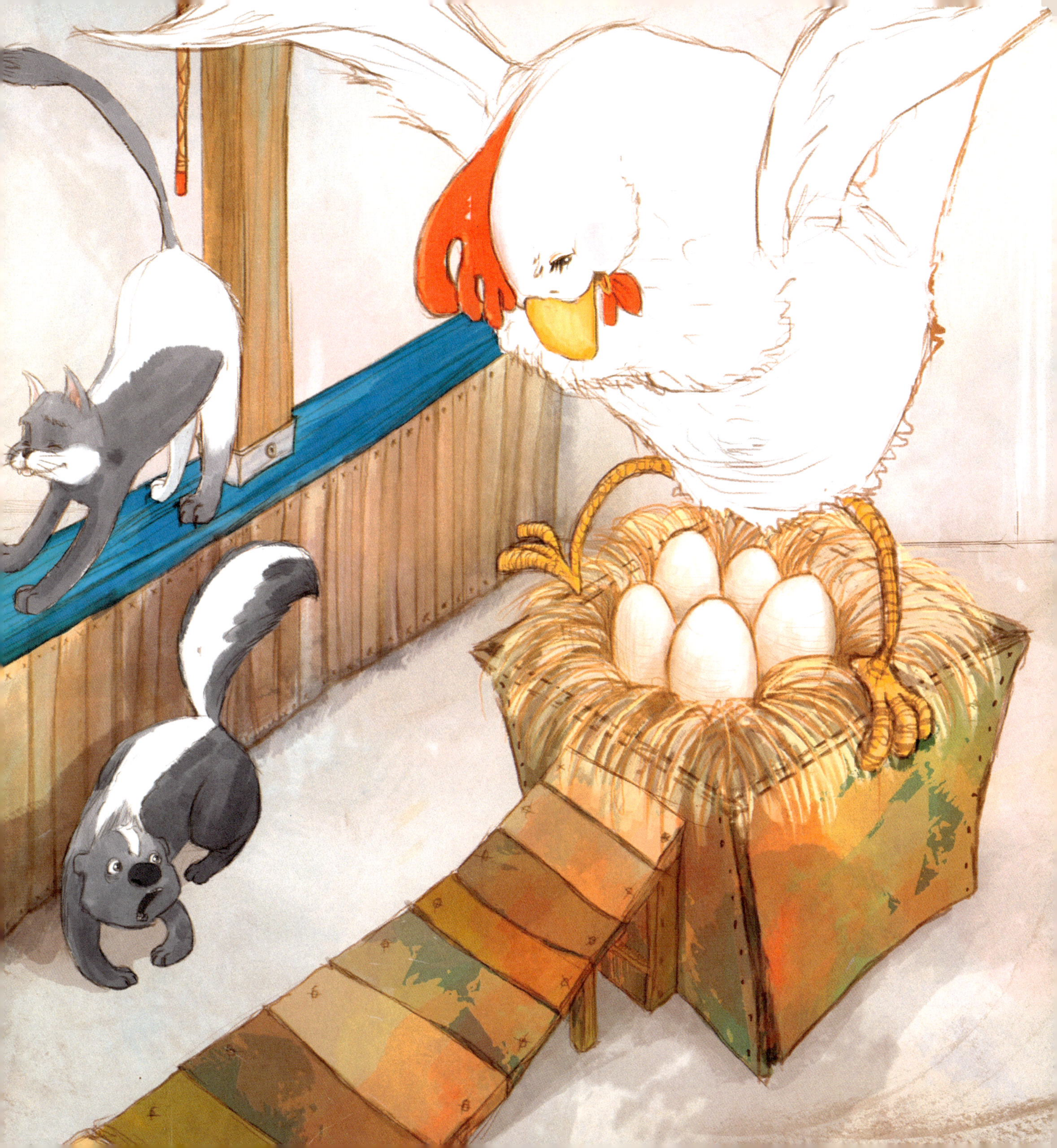

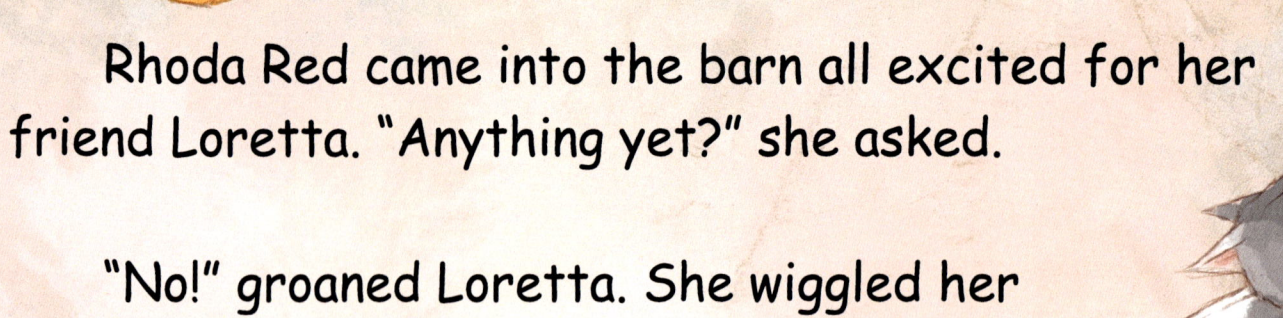

Rhoda Red came into the barn all excited for her friend Loretta. "Anything yet?" she asked.

"No!" groaned Loretta. She wiggled her bottom trying to get more comfortable. "I hope they come soon."

Rhoda couldn't wait for her friend to have chicks of her own. She looked over with pride at her own 5 chicks: Ruby, Riley, Rose, Rubin, and Roy. She knew how lucky she was to have them. She imagined how much fun the two families would have together and of course there would be more eyes to watch out for that nasty old fox!

Suddenly Loretta's eyes got big and wide. In an excited voice she yelled, "Oh my. Ohhhhh my! Something is tickling my feathers. Oh my goodness. My babies are here!"

Flying off the eggs, Loretta looked down at the nest. There, sitting amongst the hay, loose feathers, and broken egg shells, sat 5 precious baby Leghorn chicks.

Ruby, Riley, Rose, Rubin, and Roy all rushed to the edge of the nest. They were very excited to see their new friends.

"What are their names?" Rose asked.

"Everyone!" announced Loretta. "I am proud to introduce to you: Lilly, Lucy, Lola, Larry, and Lou."

Rhoda gave her friend a big hug and immediately started to advise her on how to care for her chicks. At the same time, Rhoda's chicks each took hold of one of their new friends and began to show the new buddy around the barn.

They showed them where the farmer tossed out the food for them to eat and where the best watering hole was to drink.

They showed them the difference between the black and white barn cat and the mean, stinky skunk. Most importantly, they told the new chicks to make sure to keep an eye out for the crafty old fox.

As the chicks were all getting to know each other, Rhoda was enjoying the company of her friend. She and Loretta were chatting about proper chick bedtimes, good food choices, and the importance of being on the lookout for the fox.

At the thought of the fox, Loretta looked down at the nest to make sure her children were safe, but instead of seeing her babies, all she saw was an empty nest with broken egg shells. "Oh no, no, no, no, no! They're gone!" she yelled.

Loretta cried out, "Lilly, Lucy, Lola, Larry, Lou... where are you?" She turned around, and looking around the barn, she noticed that each chick had paired, each with one of Rhoda's chicks. But were they all there?

Is the gang of 10 all there?

The older chicks looked up in surprise. "It's OK, Mrs. Leghorn," said Rubin. "We each have one of your chicks. There are 5 of us, so there are 5 of your chicks here. We're just showing your babies around the barn."

Is Rubin right? Are there 5 Leghorn chicks?

Loretta wasn't sure so she counted them. Yes! 5 Rhode Island Red chicks and 5 white Leghorn chicks. The gang was all there. "Thank goodness you're all here," said Loretta. "I'm new at being a mother and I worry about that fox your mother was telling me about."

Just then Loretta's chicks noticed that Roy had wandered off into the barnyard and was digging a big hole. They ran over to see what he was doing. He was setting another trap to catch the fox.

Ruby, Rose, Rubin, and Riley were hungry and so they went back towards the barn to see if they could find some leftover corn.

Rhoda and Loretta had been busy talking about their chicks. They looked up from the doorway of the barn.

"Oh no, no, no, no, no!" exclaimed Loretta. "Rhoda, you only have 4 chicks!"

Is the gang of 10 all there?

All the chicks turned to face their mothers. Well, all except Roy that is, because he was laying out another trap for the fox.

"Mom," the chicks all said together, "the gang's all here!"

"Phew," said Loretta. "Keeping track of these chicks is nerve-wracking."

"You have no idea," said Rhoda. "Just wait until you experience your first fox sighting. Then things can get really crazy!"

Roy walked over to the water trough to get a drink of water and got another idea about how he could capture the fox. He started drilling a hole in the side of the trough. Rose and Rubin went over to see what he was doing.

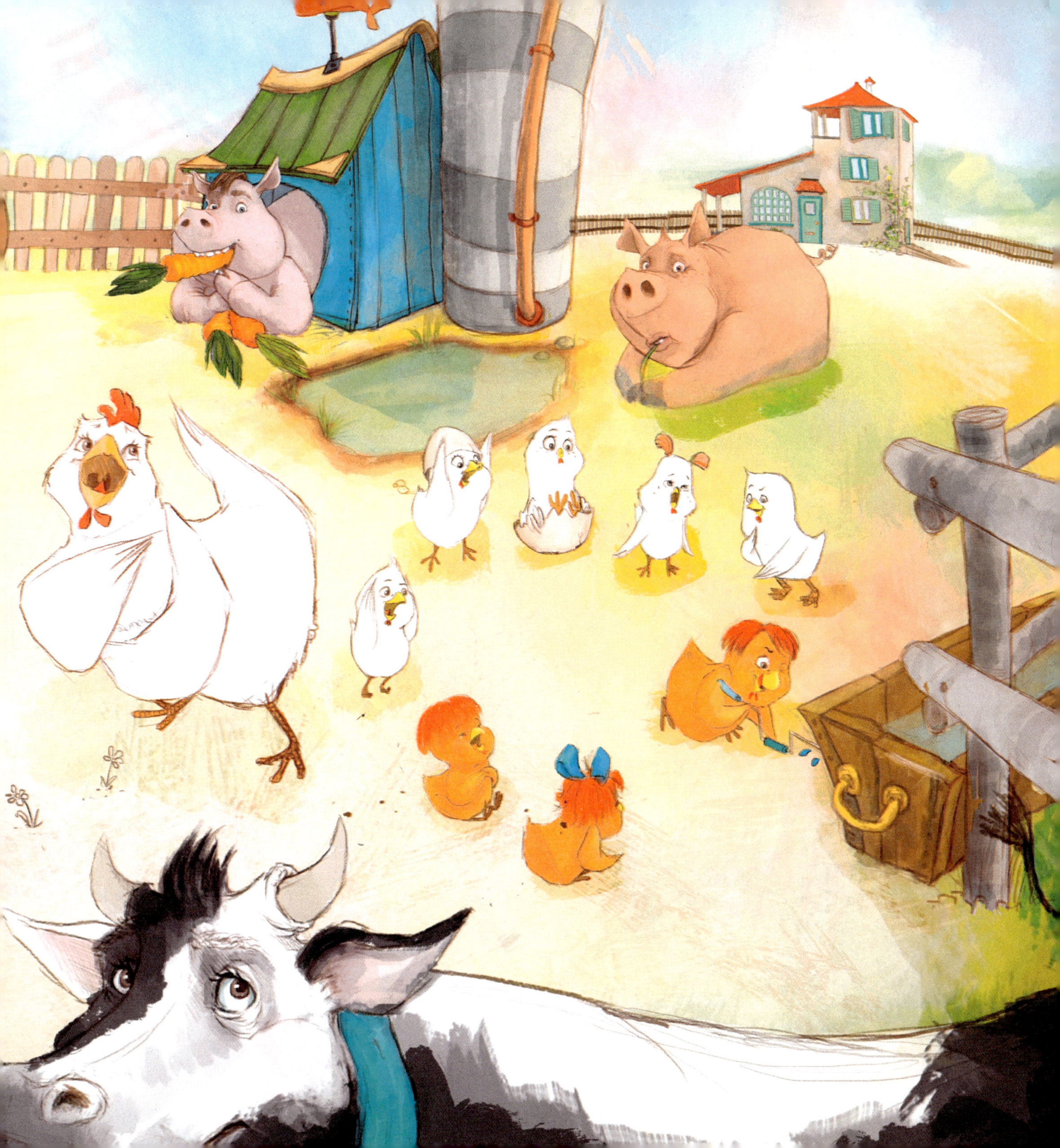

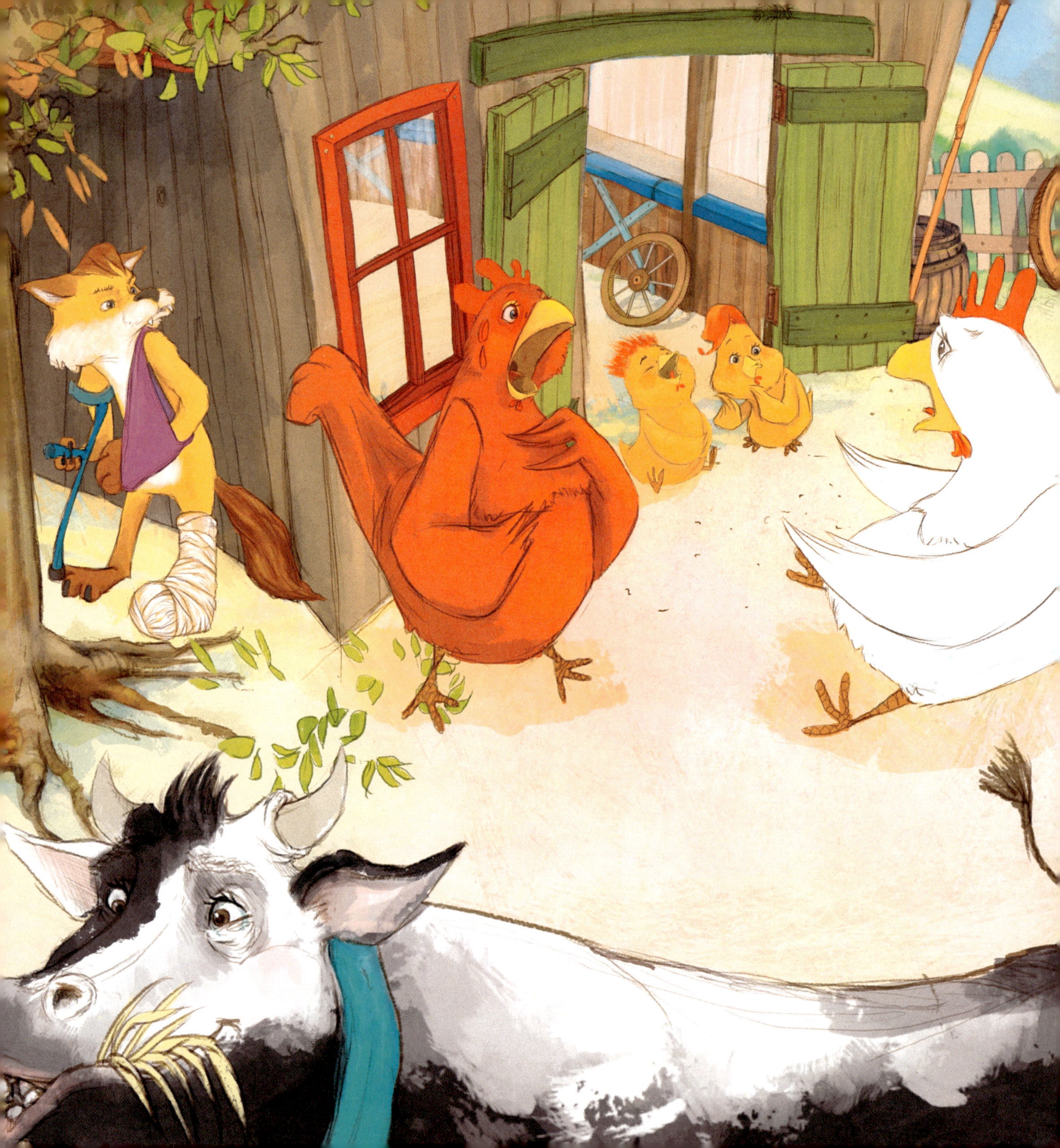

Loretta looked up and now she saw only 2 of Rhoda's chicks. "Wait... What... Where are they?" she yelled. "Oh no! Children, are you all here?"

Is the gang all here?

The chicks thought their moms' reactions were funny. Laughing, Ruby said, "We're all here. Don't worry."

Larry thought this was hilarious. "Let's do it again and see what they do this time," he said.

Lilly, Lucy, Lola, Larry, and Lou all ran toward the barn, while Riley, Rose, and Rubin hid by the cow. In order to get their moms to look, Riley pulled at the cow's tail, causing it to let out a loud, "Moooo."

Loretta and Rhoda turned at the sound of the cow. "Oh no, no, no, no, no!" exclaimed the mothers with concern. "Are all of our 10 chicks here?"

Are they?

Both moms looked on as their chicks laughed hysterically. "Alright you little rascals," said Rhoda. "No more funny business. Everyone come here."

All 10 chicks lined up near their mothers: Rhoda's 5 chicks on the left, and Loretta's 5 chicks on the right.

Rhoda tried to sound angry, but her words came out in a giggle. "We're on to you now. You can't trick us anymore."

Loretta added, "You've created all sorts of different groups, but we know now, you were all always here."

Can you think of any other ways to group the chicks?

"OK," said Rhoda. "Everyone back to the barn. It's almost dinner time and I'm hungry."

"Me too! Whew! What a day!" exclaimed Loretta. She flung open the heavy barn door to let everyone in and heard a grunt.
"What was that? Barn doors don't say Ouch!" Loretta got a little nervous and called out to Rhoda, "Are all the chicks here?"

Rhoda answered, "Let's count to be safe. Ok everyone, sound off."

"1," said Lilly.
"2," said Lucy.
"3," said Lola.
"4," said Larry.
"5," said Lou.

"Well, all 5 of my chicks are here," thought Loretta.

"6," said Ruby.
"7," said Riley.
"8," said Rose.
"9," said Rubin.

"Oh no! Where's Roy!" Rhoda yelled. "Roy, where are you?" She knew he had been trying to set traps for the fox all day. Had the fox captured him instead???

Then Rhoda saw Roy, dillydallying in the barnyard with a frustrated look on his face. She thought to herself, "....Hmmm, there are 9 already in the barn and Roy makes 1 more. That makes 10: 5 of Loretta's chicks, and 5 of my own."

As Rhoda walked over to her son, he said, "Mom, can't I stay out a little while longer? I've been setting traps for the fox all day and I haven't caught him yet."

Rhoda put her wing around Roy and said. "I know you have, my brave little chick-a-dee and I'm so proud of you. But it's getting late and it's time to come inside now. Tomorrow's another day."

As Rhoda and Roy entered the barn, Loretta started to close the heavy door for the night.
"Wait!" Loretta said, looking out. "Did you hear that?"

"Hear what?" said Rhoda. "I didn't hear anything."

"I don't know," said Loretta. "I thought I heard……."

The sun was setting over the field and the sky was a beautiful bluish, pink color with just a few wisps of clouds. Loretta looked out across the barnyard. She thought how lucky she was to be raising her baby chicks in such a beautiful, quiet, peaceful setting. With a gentle sigh Loretta said, "Nope, nothing there. Come on! Now that the gang's all here, let's eat!"

Copyright © 2018 by Mary Waesche Alessi and Cathy Fosnot

All rights reserved.

This book or any portion thereof may not be reproduced or used in any manner whatsoever without the express written permission of the publisher except for the use of brief quotations in a book review.

First Printing, 2018

ISBN-13: 978-0-9976886-9-6

Catherine Fosnot and Associates
New Perspectives on Learning, LLC
www.newperspectivesonlearning.com

About the Authors

Mary Waesche Alessi is a Registered Nurse by profession, but she also holds a degree in Early Childhood Education. With 5 preschool and kindergarten aged grandchildren, who all listen to and love her storytelling, Mary quickly discovered that she had a talent for weaving math learning opportunities into her stories with creative, fun, imaginative story lines. She currently lives in Denver, CO where she works, plays and continues to evolve as a writer of children's books.

Mary Waesche Alessi

Cathy Fosnot is Professor Emerita of Childhood Education from CCNY, where she was the founder of the acclaimed center, Mathematics in the City. She has authored numerous books and articles on mathematics education, most recently *Conferring with Young Mathematicians at Work: Making Moments Matter* and the *Contexts for Learning Mathematics* series, K-6, a curriculum used widely by schools around the world. In 2004 she received the Teacher of the Year award from CCNY. Currently she serves as the senior content consultant for the award-winning internet math environment, DreamBox Learning, and is the President of New Perspectives on Learning, New Perspectives Online, and New Perspectives on Assessment. She resides in New London, CT, where she frequently offers workshops with her team at Ocean Beach.

Cathy Fosnot

About the Illustrator

Manuela Pentangelo is an illustrator with a passion for painting and creating, leading her to have more than 40 published children's books available in many countries around the world and in many formats (print, animations, online, tablet). Her style is a combination of traditional and digital painting. She now lives and works on the island of the island, Sant'Antioco, a small island off the coast of Sardinia.

Manuela Pentangelo

Made in the USA
Columbia, SC
22 July 2021

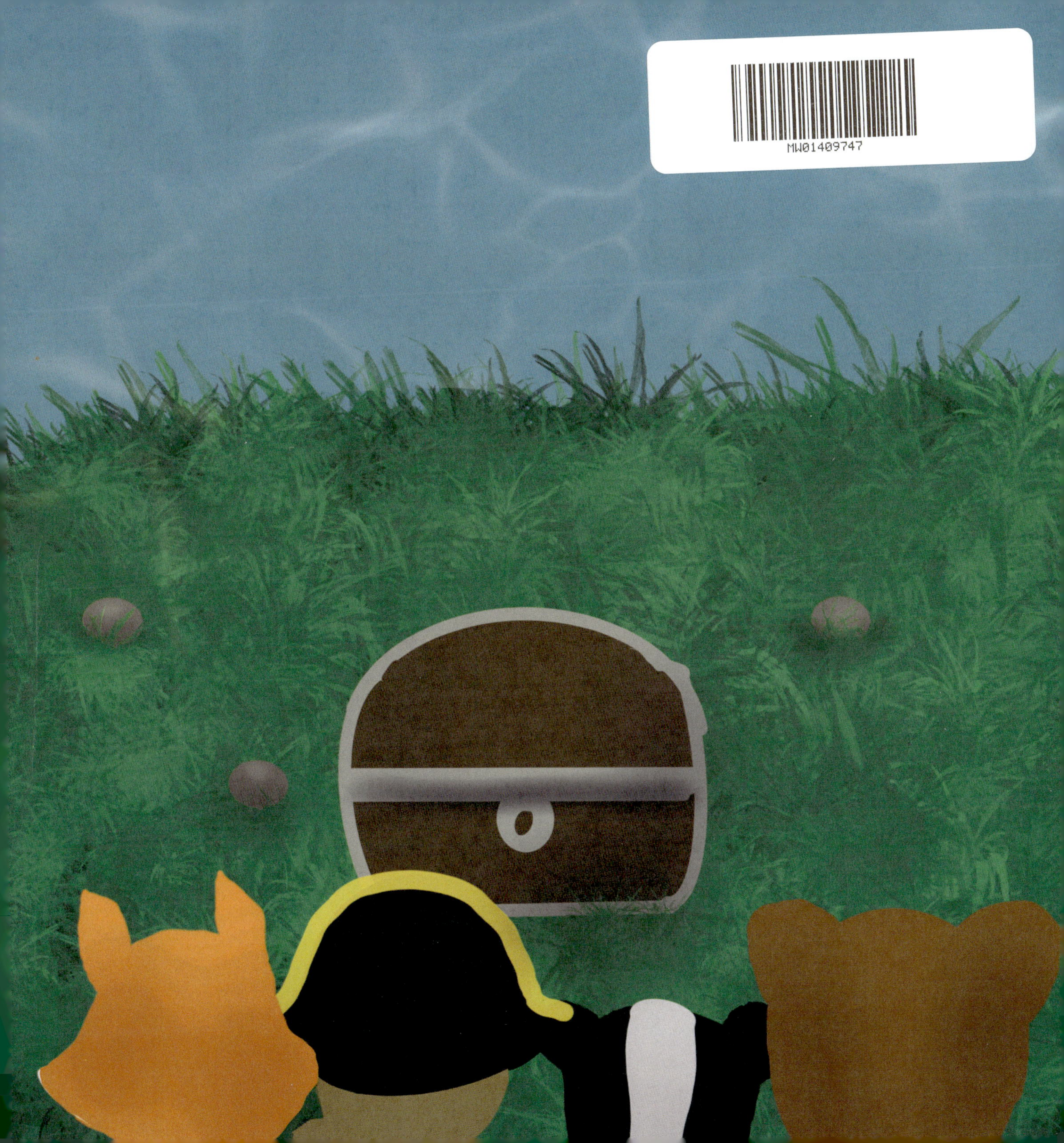

For my mom. Thank you for always being there for me.

Published by Circle Time Books, 2023
Copyright © 2023 Cazzy Zahursky/Circle Time Books, LLC
All Rights Reserved. No part of this publication may be reproduced, stored in a retrieval system or transmitted in any form by any means electronic, mechanical or photocopying, recording or otherwise without permission of author. All inquiries about this book can be sent to the author at cazzy@circletimebooks.com

Printed in the USA
Edited by Cazzy Zahusky
Paperback ISBN: 978-1-960047-00-7

Aspen Zahursky

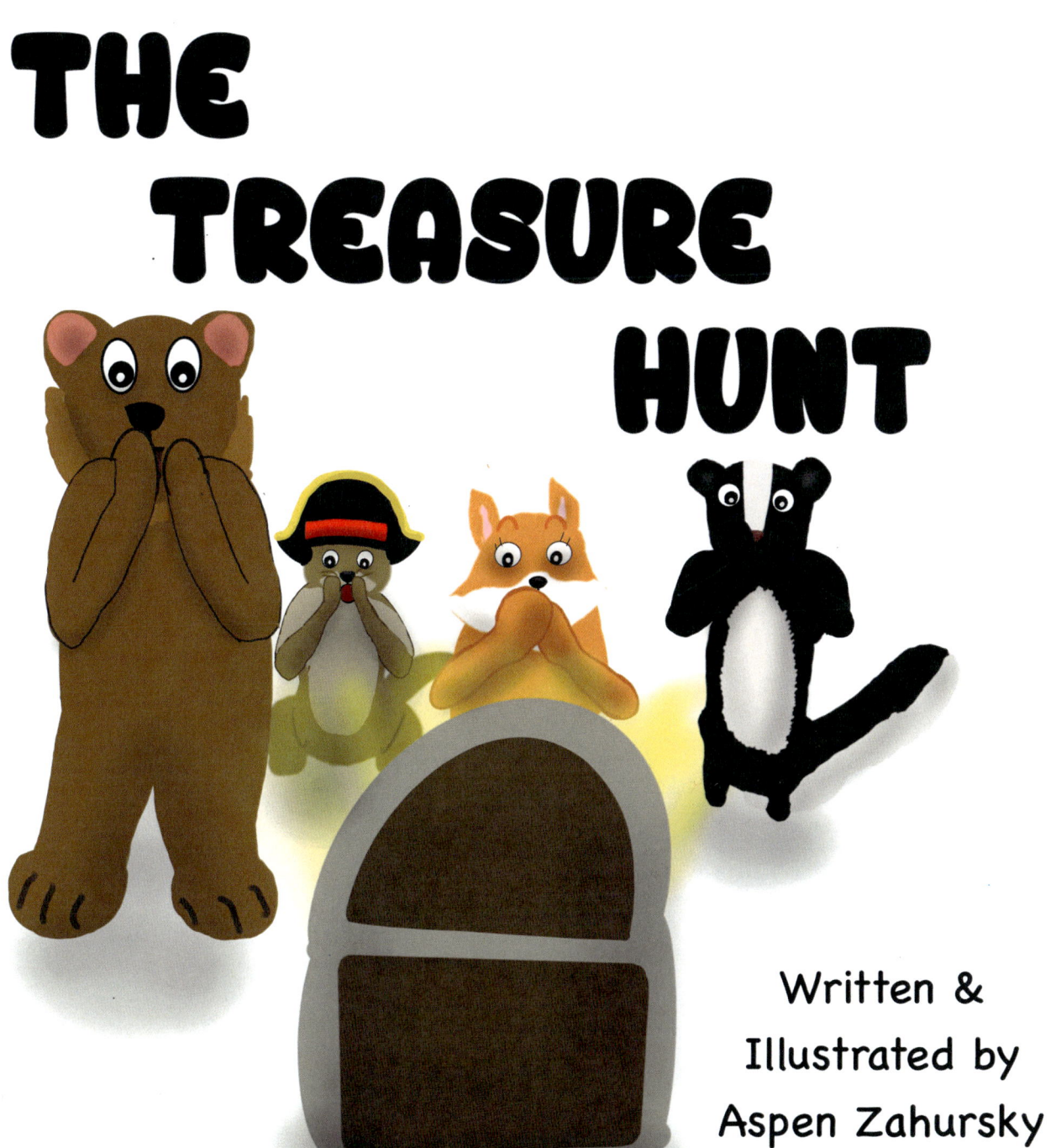

THE TREASURE HUNT

Written &
Illustrated by
Aspen Zahursky

Fox was playing in the forest by herself one morning. She was feeling bored and lonely because her family had just moved to a new part of the forest and she didn't have any friends yet.

While Fox played, she found a treasure map. She imagined the greatest treasure. She imagined a ball that she could play with.

Feeling a little unsure at first, Fox decided to follow the map.

The map took her to a grassy area where she found a skunk.

Skunk warned her, "If you come any closer, I will spray you. This is MY grassy area, get out of here."

"If you don't spray me, you can come with me to find some treasure, "said Fox.

"OK, fine. I am a little lonely. No one seems to want to be my friend because it gets a bit stinky around here. I really hope the treasure is perfume," remarked Skunk.

They both set off to find the treasure together.

The map took them to a large cave, where they met a bear.

Bear said, "This is MY cave. Skedaddle."

Skunk replied, "Let us in or I will spray you."

"No Skunk, Bear can help us find the treasure too. Bear, would you like to help find treasure with us?" Fox asked.

Bear said, "Oh fine. I guess it does get a little lonely in this big cave by myself. I sure do hope the treasure is some sweet and tasty honey."

"Well then, let's go," said Skunk. "I want to find my sweet smelling perfume."

Together Fox, Skunk, and Bear headed out to find the treasure. They finally arrived at a river.

They heard a high pitched voice say, "Arrrh, this is MY river. Scram, Mateys."

"Please let us cross the river. We are on an important mission to find treasure. You can come with us if you'd like," replied Fox.

"Oh fine, I do like myself some treasure," mumbled Otter. "I really hope the treasure is shiny stones," he continued.

Fox said, "The map shows the treasure is at the bottom of the river."

"Arrrh Mateys, I think I can get it."

Otter dove to the bottom of the river and saw a glistening treasure box. He brought it to the surface where the others were waiting for him.

Otter said, "It's my shiny rocks."
"No," Skunk said, "It's my sweet smelling perfume."
"I don't think so, I think it's my delicious honey," Bear interrupted. Fox said, "I think it will be a ball for me to play with."
"What are we waiting for, let's open it," Otter shouted.

Fox slowly opened the lid and found something gold and shiny.

Otter exclaimed, "It's a charm and there's only one. Who should get it?"
Bear suggested, "I have an idea. How about we split the charm into four pieces and we share it?"

Bear took a stone and broke the charm into four even pieces.

Bear handed out a piece of the broken charm
to each new friend.

Fox said, "The real treasure here, is our sweet friendship."
Every day after that they played together and wore their piece of the charm around their necks, proudly.

ABOUT THE AUTHOR & ILLUSTRATOR
ASPEN ZAHURSKY

Aspen is an eight-year-old author and illustrator and even though she has written many stories, The Treasure Hunt is her first published book. Aspen's other interests include soccer, gymnastics, futsol, and playing with her sister and her friends.

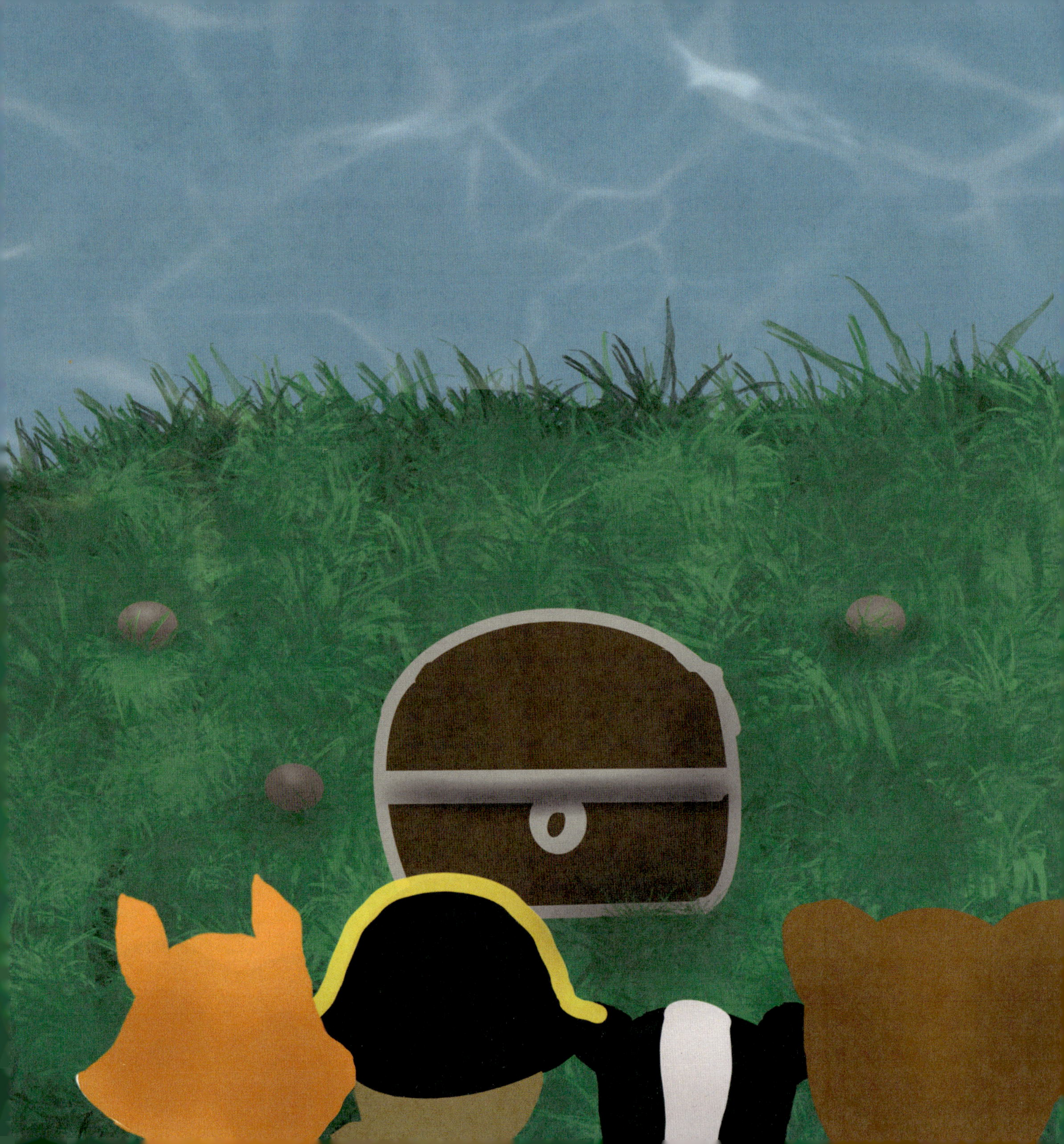

Made in the USA
Middletown, DE
23 February 2023

This Book Belongs to:

_____

To my husband, George, who has always been there for me,
encouraging and helping as I endeavored to help
strengthen the children of the Church.
—DDB

To Daniel, Jared, Josh, and Andrew;
my greatest project ever.
—KH

Text © 2019 Deanna Draper Buck

Illustrations © Karin D. Hochstrasser

All rights reserved. No part of this book may be reproduced in any form or by any means without permission in writing from the publisher, Deseret Book Company, at permissions@deseretbook.com or P. O. Box 30178, Salt Lake City, Utah 84130. This work is not an official publication of The Church of Jesus Christ of Latter-day Saints. The views expressed herein are the responsibility of the author and do not necessarily represent the position of the Church or of Deseret Book Company.

DESERET BOOK is a registered trademark of Deseret Book Company.

Visit us at DeseretBook.com

Library of Congress Cataloging-in-Publication Data
Names: Buck, Deanna Draper, author. | Hochstrasser, Karin, illustrations.
Title: The whole armor of God / Deanna Draper Buck ; illustrated by Karin Hochstrasser.
Description: Salt Lake City, Utah : Deseret Book, [2019].
Identifiers: LCCN 2018047215 | ISBN 9781629725772 (hardbound : alk. paper)
Subjects: LCSH: Armor—Juvenile literature. | Spiritual warfare—Juvenile literature. | Mormon children—Conduct of life—Juvenile literature. | Mormon children—Religious life—Juvenile literature. | The Church of Jesus Christ of Latter-day Saints—Juvenile literature. | Picture books for children. | LCGFT: Picture books.
Classification: LCC BX8656 .B83 2019 | DDC 242/.62—dc23
LC record available at https://lccn.loc.gov/2018047215

Printed in China
RR Donnelley, Shenzhen, China   03/2019

10 9 8 7 6 5 4 3 2 1

THE WHOLE ARMOR OF GOD

Written by
DEANNA DRAPER BUCK

Illustrated by
KARIN HOCHSTRASSER

DESERET BOOK

Salt Lake City, Utah

We lived in the spirit world with Heavenly Father before we were born. He loves us and created this beautiful world so that we could come to earth, get a body, and learn how to be like Him.

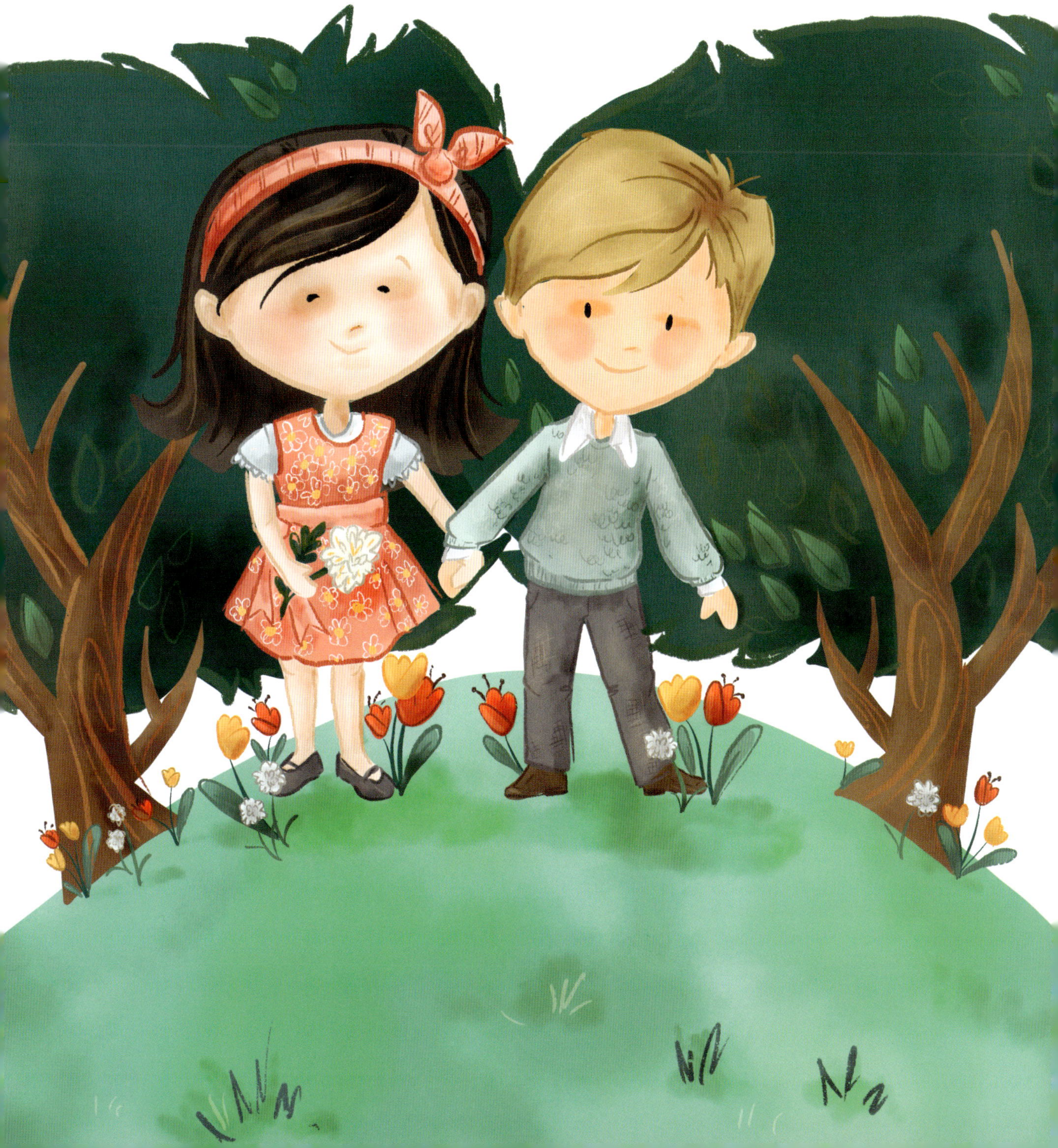

Heavenly Father knew that we would be tested and tempted, and so He gave us THE ARMOR OF GOD to help us keep our spirits safe.

The first piece of armor goes around your waist like a belt.
It is called the GIRDLE OF TRUTH.

Testimony

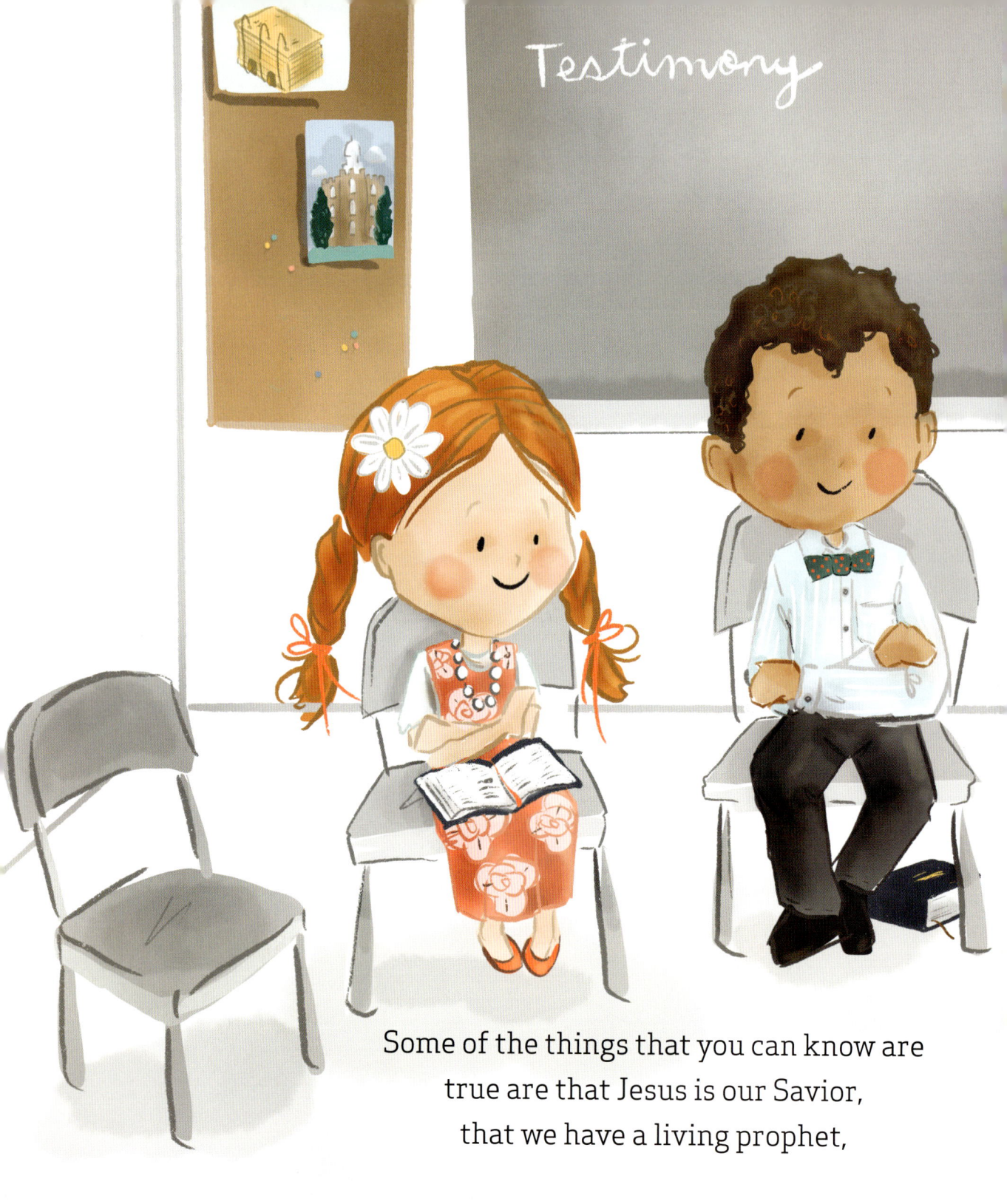

Some of the things that you can know are true are that Jesus is our Savior, that we have a living prophet, and that the Book of Mormon is true. When you know what is true, you can make good choices and be happy.

The **BREASTPLATE OF RIGHTEOUSNESS** goes on your chest over your heart.

breastplate of righteousness

Righteousness is the good and kind things you think, say, and do.

When we love Heavenly Father with all our hearts, we will want to be righteous, obey His commandments, and help others.

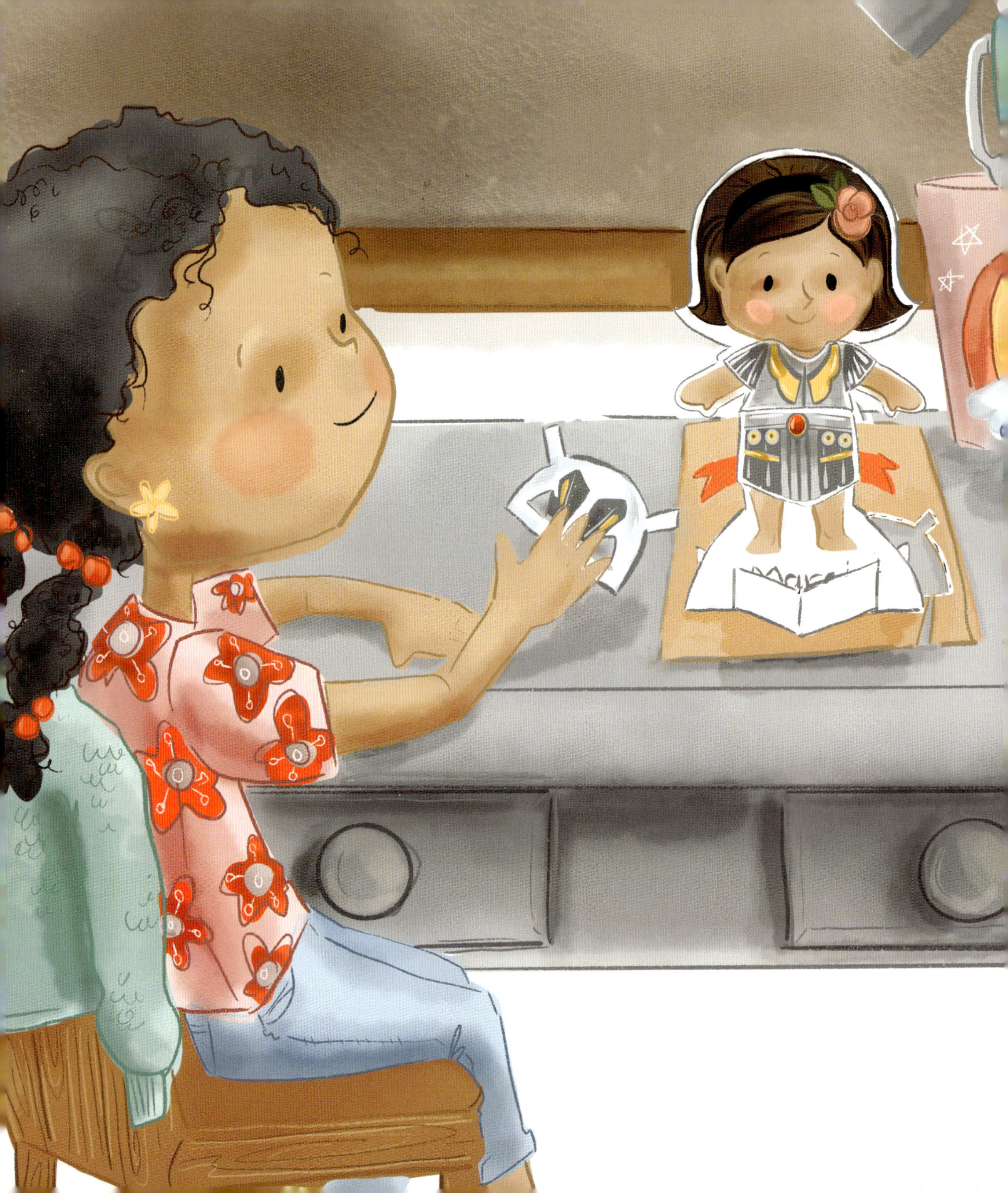

The armor for your feet is called the **PREPARATION OF THE GOSPEL OF PEACE**.

You prepare to be like Jesus by learning about Him. Then you follow in His peaceful footsteps by sharing, taking turns, quickly obeying your parents, and not fighting.

When you are prepared, you can share the gospel of peace by being a good example to others.

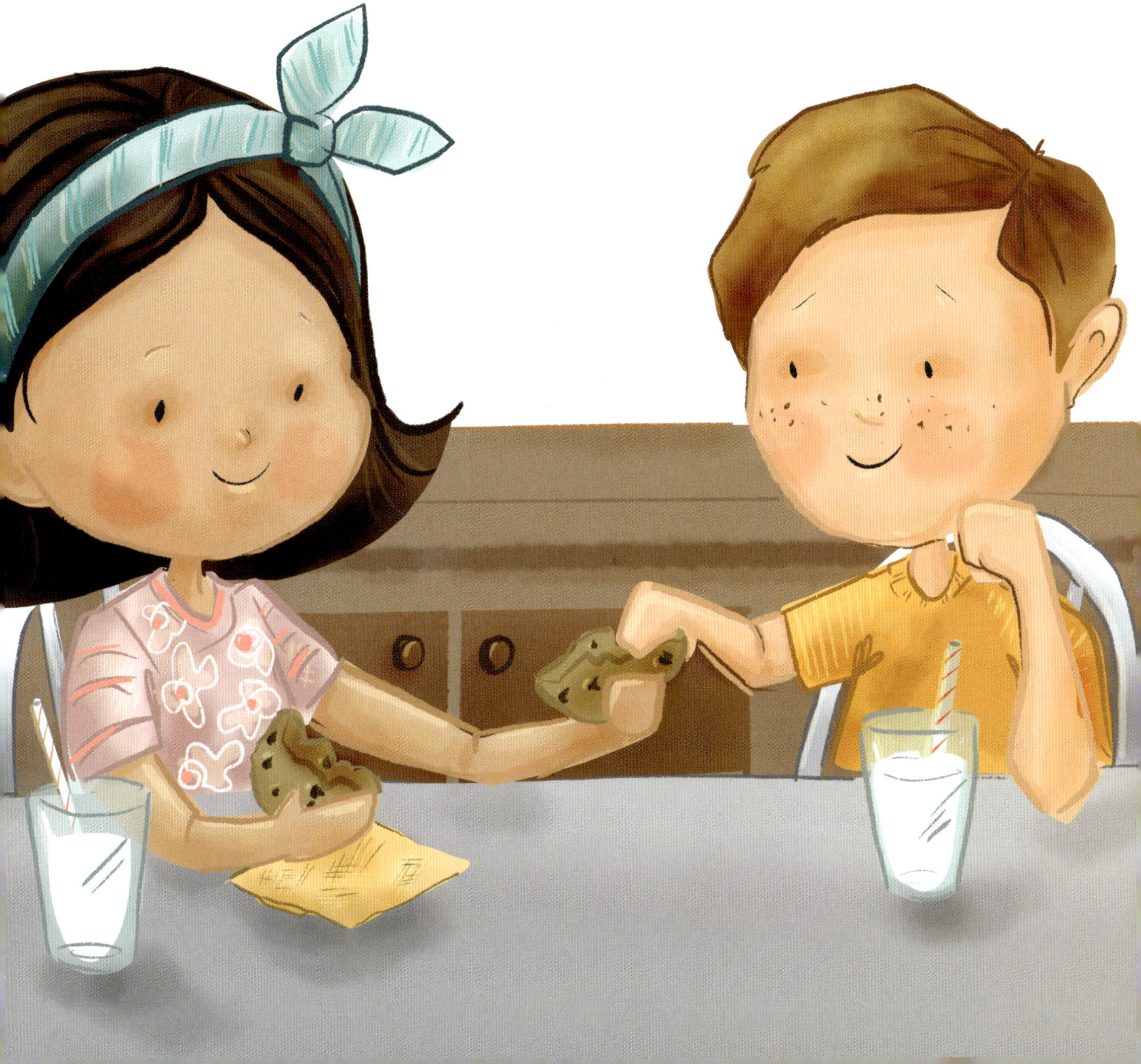

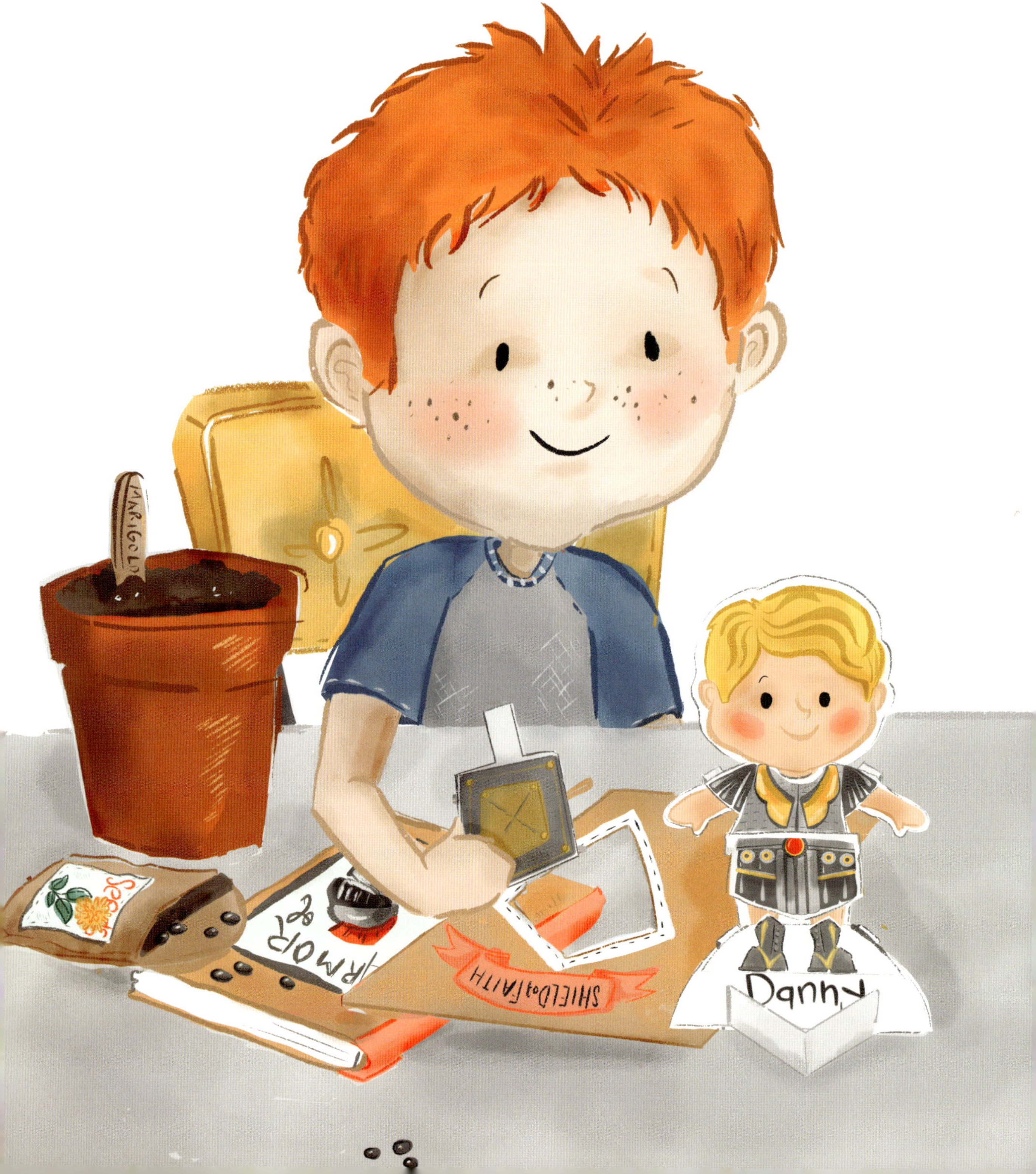
Seeds
SHIELD of FAITH
Danny

The **SHIELD OF FAITH** goes on your arm. Faith means to believe and trust in something that you cannot see.

Even though you can't see Heavenly Father, you can have faith that He will hear and answer your prayers when you are sad, angry, disappointed, or even frightened.

When you have faith, God will help and comfort you.

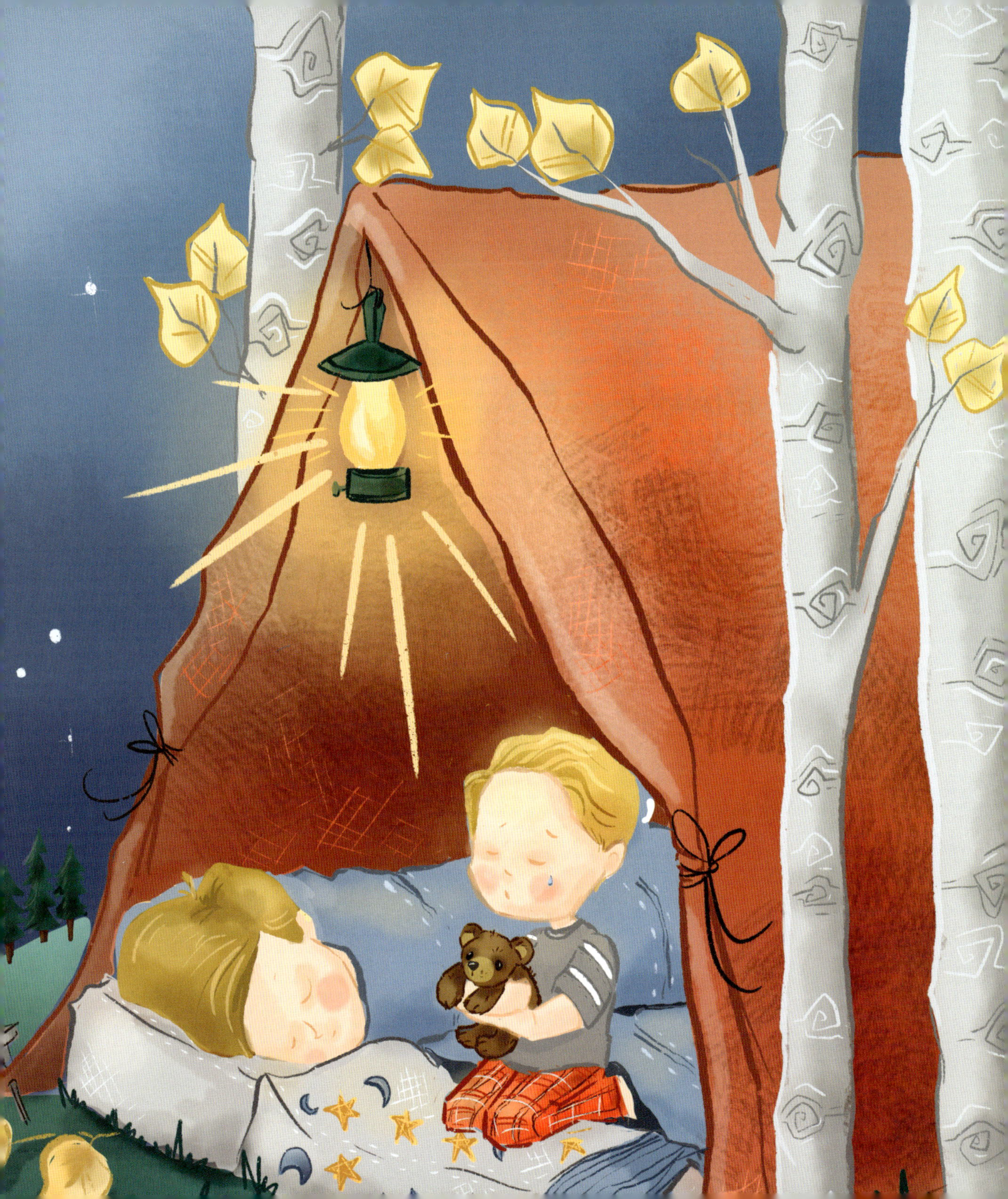

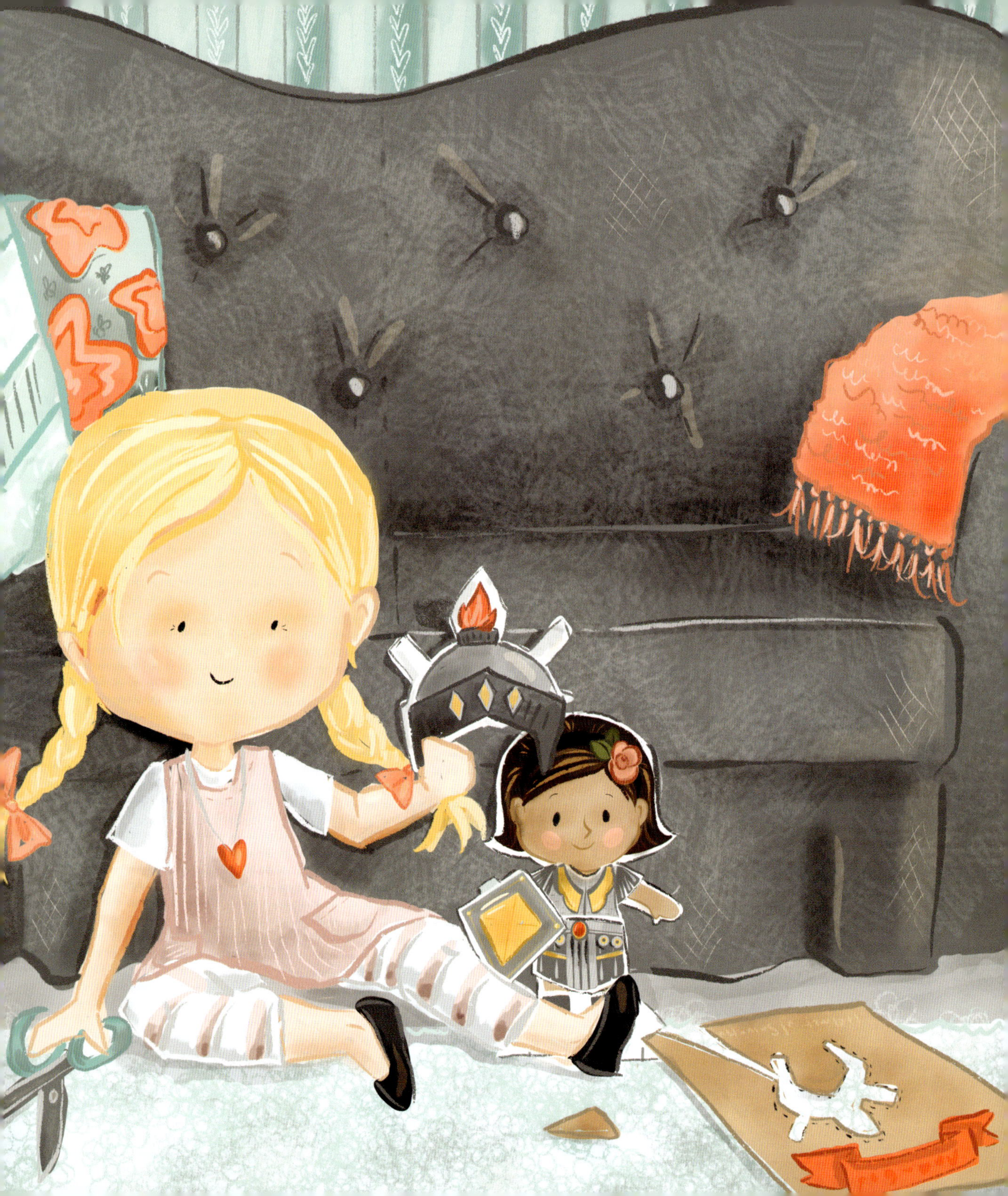

With the **HELMET OF SALVATION** on your head, you can remember that Jesus is your Savior. Salvation means to help or save. Sometimes you will make mistakes or do something that is wrong.

Because Jesus is our Savior, He makes it possible to repent and be forgiven.

You can say that you are sorry and try to do better next time.

When you repent or forgive others,
you will feel happy and peaceful inside.

The last piece of armor is the SWORD OF THE SPIRIT, which is the Holy Ghost.

The Holy Ghost is so powerful that He is able to help people want to change and do better.

When you are eight years old, you can be baptized and receive the gift of the Holy Ghost.

The Holy Ghost reminds you of the promises you made when you were baptized and will guide you as you make choices.

Every day when you pray, you can thank Heavenly Father for all of your blessings.

You can ask Heavenly Father to help you remember what is TRUE, to choose the RIGHT, to bring PEACE and joy to your home by sharing and being helpful, to have FAITH in Jesus, to remember that Jesus is our SAVIOR, and to listen to the HOLY GHOST.

When we have on the **WHOLE ARMOR OF GOD**, we will be strong, safe, happy, and ready to fight on the Lord's side!

ABOUT THE AUTHOR

Award-winning, best-selling author Deanna Draper Buck and her husband have been married for fifty years. They currently live in Hooper, Utah, where they enjoy gardening and entertaining their eight children, twenty-five grandchildren, and one great-grandchild. Deanna also enjoys quilting. She has written fifteen LDS children's books, explaining gospel principles, Church history, and scripture stories in a simplified style.

ABOUT THE ILLUSTRATOR

Karin D. Hochstrasser has a bachelor of fine arts in illustration from Brigham Young University and a love of creativity. Whether she's mini baking, party planning, sewing, or drawing, her trademark whimsical style follows her wherever she goes. Her playful approach to portraits has gained her Etsy shop, *Ink Puddles by Karin*, a devoted following. She has had her work showcased throughout her community as well as in the Harris Fine Arts Center at BYU. As a devoted mother of four boys, her frequent interactions with children and youth give her art an authentic quality that resonates naturally with young audiences.